52
PRESCHOOL
CRAFTS

written by Joanna R. Hart

illustrated by Russell Rigo

STANDARD PUBLISHING
Cincinnati, Ohio   2105

ISBN: 0-87239-725-4

©1984. The STANDARD PUBLISHING Company, Cincinnati, Ohio
Division of STANDEX INTERNATIONAL Corporation
Printed in U.S.A.   **2105**

TABLE OF CONTENTS

READY-SET-GO 5

JANUARY
God's Numbers 6
Snowflakes 6
Peanut Bird Feeder 7
Blooming Pretzel Plaque 7
Jesus and the Children Belt 8

FEBRUARY
Heart Pin 9
Happy Heart Mobile 10
Wallet 11
My Family Van 12

MARCH
Mission Air Station 12
Airplanes 13
Find My Sheep 14
Egg Basket 15

APRIL
Bunny Place Card 16
In Jesus' Footprints 17
Wall Hanging Banner 18
Peel the Banana Book 18
Circle Animals 19

MAY
Sharing Basket 20
Mother's Day Card 21
Tea for You 22
Sailor Hat 23

JUNE
Father's Bookmark 23
Father's Day Card 24
Tracings 25
Witness Magnet 25

JULY

Patriotic Pennant 26
Salad Faces 27
Chinese Hat 28
Key Scriptures.. 29
Diamond Pendant.. 29

AUGUST

Shoe Box Church 30
Pixie Hat 31
Daytime Sky Poster 32
Rubbings... 33

SEPTEMBER

Apple Prayer Reminder... 33
Helping Hands.. 34
Noah's Animals 35
Flower Lei 36

OCTOBER

Praise the Lord Harp 37
Scarecrow Puppet 38
A Great Fish 38
Sea Poster 39
Decorating Chains 40

NOVEMBER

Smiling Face Hand Puppet 41
Tepee.. 41
"Eyes" Book 42
Thanksgiving Turkey Cookies 43

DECEMBER

Space Poster 44
Christmas Wreath Name Plate 45
Story Scroll 46
Christmas Card Puppets 46

READY - SET - GO

READY: Under this heading for each craft you will find the *materials and the tools* you will need for each craft.

SET: Under this heading you will read the things that you, *the teacher,* will have to do to get "set" to start the craft.

GO: Under this heading you will find what *the children* will do, with your supervision, to complete the craft.

GLUING: For crafts calling for the application of glue, do not make it available until ready to use it. Cut apart egg cups from a foam egg carton. Put a little glue in egg cup and apply to craft with a cotton swab. Another method of applying glue is to put glue into small, empty nose-spray bottles. The hole is small allowing only a dot of glue to squeeze out at a time. The bottles are small, making it easy for little hands to handle.

CUTTING: Children can learn to use scissors by a simple exercise used several weeks in succession. Give each child several strips of contruction paper 12" x 1" and an envelope. With blunt scissors let them cut the strips into "tickets" and place in the envelope. When they can cut easily, give them a wider strip to make the tickets. Soon they will be ready for a simple object to cut.

COLORING: Start children with large crayons on large objects. At first there is nothing but scribbles; but as they practice, they will change their style. As they learn to color, they also learn about mixing colors to make new colors.

GOD'S NUMBERS

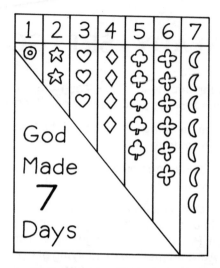

READY: 7" x 11" pieces of cardboard, a box of frosted oat cereal with marshmallow bits, glue, felt-tip marker and crayons.

SET: Adapt this craft to any Bible story with numbers. With felt-tip marker, put numbers across top, and lines up and down to separate each of the rows of cereal. Add appropriate words for children to trace.

GO: Place a different cereal under each number, making sure you have counted correctly. Glue cereal in place. Trace words with crayons.

SNOWFLAKES

READY: 9" x 12" dark blue construction paper, 5" white paper doilies, scissors, and glue.

SET: Using two doilies for each child, cut or tear out the large round designs. You can cut or tear several at one time. With a white crayon, print "Thank You, God, for snow" on each sheet of dark blue paper.

GO: Using a small amount of glue in an egg cup and a cotton swab, place dots of glue at random on the dark blue paper. Then put the snowflakes in place. Let dry. Decorate a wall or a bulletin board.

PEANUT BIRD FEEDER

READY: Long darning needles, fish line, scissors, peanuts in the shell and some for eating, too.

SET: Thread about 18″ of fish line into needles.

GO: Thread 6 or 8 peanuts onto line at smallest part of peanut. remove needle and tie ends together. Attach to a tree at your house for the birds to eat.

BLOOMING PRETZEL PLAQUE

READY (for each plaque): 9″ heavy paper plate, 4 small pretzels, 1 large pretzel, 3½ pretzel sticks, paper punch, glue, felt-tip marker, ribbon, and broken pretzels for nibbling.

SET: Put out all materials on a newspaper-topped table.

GO: With a felt-tip marker, print "Thank You, God, for beautiful flowers" around the rim of the plate. Glue the back side of 1½ pretzel sticks and put down the center of the plate, leaving room at the top for the large pretzel. Glue large pretzel in place. Glue on four 1/2 sticks for stems for the leaves. Glue on leaves. Punch hole at top of plate and attach ribbon for hanging.

NOTE: This craft makes an excellent gift for fathers, or other men you may wish to honor. Change the printed message accordingly ("Thank You, God, for my dad," etc.).

JESUS AND THE CHILDREN BELT

READY: Lightweight cardboard, scissors, 40" shoestrings, paper punch, reinforcements, and the Christ seals #1943, Children of the World seals #1748, or Child Activity seals #1940. (Available from your Christian bookstore or Standard Publishing.)

SET: Cut six 2" circles for each student from lightweight cardboard.

GO: Punch two holes on each side of the circles. Thread the two shoestrings into the holes crossing them between circles. Stick Jesus seals and children seals on the circles. Tie at the ends and wear as a belt.

HEART PIN

READY: 6″ x 6″ pieces of red construction paper, felt-tip pens, 5″ x 5″ pieces of white construction paper, scissors, 12″ pieces of pink ribbon, glue, head of Christ seals (#1943, available at your Christian bookstore or from Standard Publishing), and small safety pins.

SET: Make two hearts for each child (one red 6″ across and one white 5″). On the bottom edge of the red heart, print "Love each other, as I have loved you" (John 15:12). (See illustration.) Cut ribbon in 12″ pieces.

GO: Glue the two hearts together with a piece of pink ribbon between making a loop at the top. Place a seal in the center. When the glue is dry, pin it on you with a small safety pin.

HAPPY HEART MOBILE

READY: Styrofoam meat trays, red felt-tip pen, scissors, glue, paper punch, red yarn, red fringe balls, and plastic lids (cottage cheese or whipped topping).

SET: Cut 3 hearts 2″ x 2″ from a meat tray. On one of the hearts print the Bible verse, "Happy are the pure in heart" (Matthew 5:8).

Cut yarn in 12", 9", and 6" lengths. Tie a 12", a 9", and a 6" length of yarn to a ring cut from a plastic cottage cheese or whipped topping lid. Tie another 12" piece of yarn for hanging.

GO: Punch holes and attach yarn to hearts. Glue on faces made with red fringe balls for eyes and a small piece of red yarn curved and glued on for mouth. Hang in a breeze.

WALLET

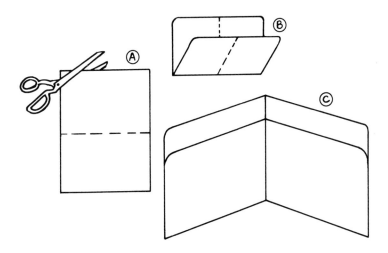

READY: Suede cloth or brown construction paper, glue, scissors, felt-tip marker, seals, and play money, invitation or announcement.

SET: Cut wallet from suede cloth or construction paper to measure 7" x 6". Fold up leaving 1/2" more on back side. Print the child's name in one corner. On the back side print: "God loves a cheerful giver" (2 Corinthians 9:7).

GO: Glue ends to form a wallet. Place seals on outside. Insert play money or an invitation to a meeting or party, or an appeal for a very special missionary project.

MY FAMILY VAN

READY: Paper for drawing and coloring, lightweight cardboard, pencils, crayons, and scissors (optional).

SET: Make patterns for van (8″ x 4″), tires, and windows from the lightweight cardboard.

GO: Draw around the patterns to make a van. Make as many windows as you have family members. Color the van, all except the windows. Draw the members of your family in the windows. If desired, cut out van. On the back, print this Bible verse: "We will serve the Lord" (Joshua 24:15).

MISSION AIR STATION

READY: 18″ squares of corrugated cardboard, shoe boxes, oatmeal boxes or milk cartons (1 quart size), scissors, felt-tip marker, glue and spray paint (optional).

SET: Cover work area with newspapers. The 18″ square of corrugated cardboard will be the base. Cut the side out of the shoe box for the hanger.

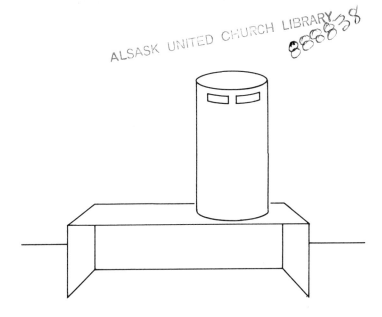

GO: Glue the open-sided shoe box to the back of the base. With help from your teacher cut some observation windows near the top of the oatmeal box or milk carton and glue it on one end of the shoe box for your observation tower. Spray paint. Use as a base for your airplanes (see below).

NOTE: As children work on this craft, talk about missionaries who fly to different parts of the world to tell about Jesus. On the top of the oatmeal box, print this Bible verse: "Go into all the world and preach the good news" (Mark 16:15). (If using a milk carton, print Bible verse on a piece of construction paper, and glue to the top.)

AIRPLANES

READY: Non-spring wooden clothespins, tongue depressors, golf tees, small saw, glue, spray paint (optional), and sandpaper.

SET: Cover work area with newspapers. For the jet plane, saw tongue depressors in half at an angle.

GO: For jet plane, glue the two parts of the tongue depressor in the slot of the clothespin (see illustration). Sand off the point of a golf tee and glue to nose of clothespin. Insert two golf tees at tail.

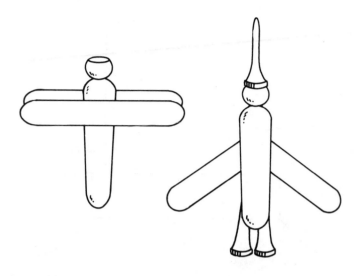

For biplane—glue two tongue depressors to clothespin as wings. You may spray paint them if you wish. Store airplanes in mission air station (see page 12).

NOTE: As children "fly" their planes, talk about Jesus' command to "Go and make disciples of all nations" (Matthew 28:19).

FIND MY SHEEP

READY: Sandpaper, fake fur in black and white, scissors, dots punched from white paper, and glue.

SET: Make sheep pattern from sandpaper. Using pattern, cut two bodies and four feet for each sheep from black and white fake fur.

GO: Glue feet, wrong sides together. Glue to the body between front and back. Glue front body to back body with wrong sides together. Glue head on center of body and glue eyes on head.

NOTE: It is fun to collect all sheep, hide them in the room and let the children find them. If desired, make one sheep in a different color to be the prize sheep.

When all of the sheep are found, share with the children this Bible verse: "Jesus said, 'I am the good shepherd'" (John 10:7, 11). Jesus loves all of His sheep (every person on the earth). He does not want anyone to be lost.

EGG BASKET

READY: 1/2 gallon cardboard milk cartons, razor cutter, crayons, construction paper, scissors, glue, spoons, potting soil, rye grass seed, water, hard-boiled eggs, stapler, and felt-tip markers.

SET: Cut carton as shown before class time. Cut two pieces of construction paper for each carton: one piece to wrap around sides and one to cover handle. Spread work area with newspapers.

GO: Cover carton with construction paper and glue in place. Decorate as desired. Fill carton with potting soil. Slowly add water and mix until all is damp. (Carton should be filled to 1½" from top.) Sow thickly with grass seed. Keep moist until grass stands above top of basket. Staple handle and cover with construction paper. Place eggs on top of grass. Print on a 3" x 2" card these words: "God will take care of you!" Put card in the basket and share with a sick friend.

NOTE: Alternate idea—After carton is decorated, glue Styrofoam square to inside bottom of carton. Fill with flowers. (Secure flowers by putting the stems in the Styrofoam.)

BUNNY PLACE CARD

READY: Lightweight cardboard in a pastel color, scissors, curly ribbon, paper punch, marshmallow bunnies, and felt-tip marker.

SET: Cut an egg shape from a piece of cardboard 2½" x 4". Stand by to assist in tying bunny to card.

GO: Write your name at the top of the card. Punch two holes, thread curly ribbon through holes, and tie bunny to card. Ribbon should be around bunny's neck. Curl ribbon. Trim bottom to make bunny stand.

NOTE: Use this craft for a party or as a take-home treat. As the children are working, ask them to share why they like springtime. Lead them in thanking God for spring flowers and animals.

IN JESUS' FOOTPRINTS

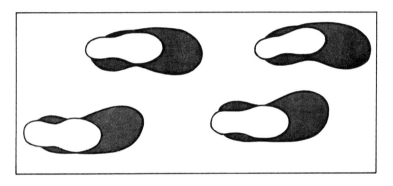

READY: Pieces of sandpaper 4½" x 11" (half of a large sheet), scissors, paper punch, yarn, glue, and two shades of colored construction paper.

SET: For each child, cut four shoe prints 1¼" x 3½" from the darker paper and four shoe prints 1" x 2¼" from the lighter paper. Cut out a 2" x 1½" piece of construction paper. Print "Jesus said, 'Follow Me.'" (Matthew 9:9).

GO: Punch a hole at top of sandpaper and insert yarn for hanging. Glue the four large prints on the sandpaper as though they were walking. Then glue the four small prints on top of the large ones. In the lower left corner, glue the Bible words. Imagine that the large prints belong to Jesus and the small ones belong to you.

WALL HANGING BANNER

READY: 12" x 15" sheets from a wallpaper book, 1/2 sheets of same kind of paper in contrasting colors, yarn, glue, masking tape, plastic straws, scissors, and seals (optional).

SET: For each banner cut a cross 6" wide and 8" tall from the contrasting color of wallpaper.

GO: Fold down about 1½" on 12" side of large piece of wallpaper. Glue this heading only on the edge or tape down with masking tape. When glue is dry insert a 36" piece of colorful yarn. Also center a plastic drinking straw in the heading for stability. Tie yarn for hanging. Glue cross to center of wall hanging. If desired, place large seal in center of cross. If no seal is used, print the words "Live for Jesus" on the wall hanging banner.

PEEL THE BANANA BOOK

READY: Yellow construction paper, white typing paper, scissors, paper punch, crayons, chicken rings, reinforcements, and glue.

"The Lord is my helper" Hebrews 13:6.

SET: Cut out a banana book, using yellow construction paper for the peel (cover) and white typing paper for the pages. Write or type memory verses on typing paper and cut out for children to glue in banana book.

GO: With a crayon, add markings to yellow construction paper banana. Assemble books and punch a hole at the top of the peel and each page. Reinforce holes with reinforcements. Fasten with chicken ring. Glue one memory verse to each page.

NOTE: This book can be enlarged as children learn more memory verses.

CIRCLE ANIMALS

READY: Scraps of colored construction paper, 9″ x 12″ pieces of paper for mounting circle animals, glue, scissors, and reinforcements.

SET: Cut out circles measuring 4½″ to ½″ in diameter. Make some half circles. Complete several circle animals for samples. (Some children will want to create animals of their own.) On the pieces of paper used to mount animals, print this Bible verse:

"God saw all that he had made, and it was very good" (Genesis 1:31).

GO: Arrange circles on your paper to form the animal of your choice. When your animal is completely formed, glue down all pieces.

SHARING BASKET

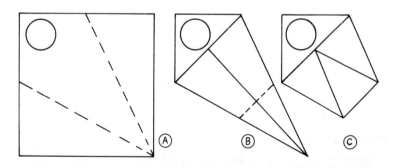

READY: 9″ squares of light colored construction paper, ruler, pencil, scissors, tape, and crayons.

SET: With a ruler and pencil, make dotted lines for folding. Cut a hole for hanging on doorknob. On the back of the sharing basket lightly print this Bible verse: Jesus said, "I am with you always" (Matthew 28:20).

GO: Decorate basket with crayons. Trace over the Bible words on the back. Fold on dotted lines, then fold point at bottom up, so all points meet. Tape securely. Fill with flowers, wrapped candy or homemade cookies. Hang it on a doorknob to give someone a delightful surprise.

MOTHER'S DAY CARD

READY: 11½" x 11½" white or pastel construction paper, 12" white doilies, scissors, glue, large movable eyes, red heart seals or red hearts made from construction paper, white or colored ribbon, paper punch, and felt-tip pens.

SET: Fold construction paper in half. Fold a white paper doily in half, matching scallops. Place construction paper inside the doily. Cut construction paper to shape of doily. On the inside left-hand page, print "To a wonderful Mom."

GO: Glue around edge of doily. Inside glue a large movable eye and a red heart seal, and print the letter "U". Print your name.

Punch two holes on the scalloped side and tie a ribbon to close your card.

TEA FOR YOU

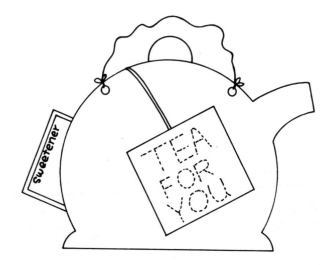

READY: Light-colored construction paper, yarn, tea bags, packets of sweetener, tape, scissors, fine felt-tip marker, crayons, 2" x 2" cards, and glue.

SET: Fold construction paper in half. Cut out double teapot. (Fold of paper should be bottom of teapot.) On the 2" x 2" card dot to dot, "Tea for You."

GO: Decorate teapot with crayons. On one side of the teapot print, "Love one another" (John 13:35). Punch holes as shown. Make a handle by tying an 8" piece of yarn in holes. Place a tea bag inside, letting string from it hang down outside. Tape sweetener inside pot. Glue 2" x 2" card to tea bag string. With fine felt-tip marker fill in the dot-to-dot letters. Give it to your grandma or mother for Mother's Day.

SAILOR HAT

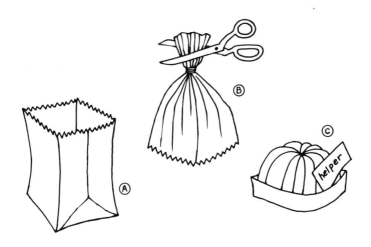

READY: White lunch bags, scissors, rubber bands, card, and felt-tip marker.

SET: Turn sack wrong side out. Twist at closed end and secure with a rubber band. Cut away excess sack close to rubber band. Turn right side out.

GO: Turn up open end of sack two times to form brim. Place a corner of a card in the brim, glueing it to hold in place. Use as a name tag, or a helper's tag.

NOTE: This craft correlates with Paul's shipwreck (Acts 27). If possible, let the children make their hats before the Bible story time so they can wear the hats during the story.

FATHER'S BOOKMARK

READY: Construction paper, crayons, scissors, and yarn.

SET: Cut four ties for each child (5" x 2¼"). Print "Be Strong in the Lord " (Ephesians 6:10) on one tie.

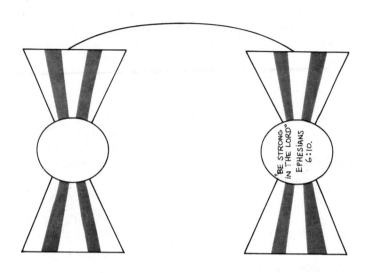

GO: Color the ties on one side. Glue two ties with the wrong sides together on each end of a 9" piece of colored yarn.

FATHER'S DAY CARD

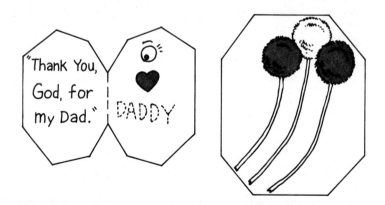

READY: Construction paper, yarn, colored balls from ball fringe, large movable eye, heart seals or hearts made from red construction paper, scissors, felt-tip pen, and glue.

SET: Fold an 8½" x 5½" piece of construction paper into a 4¼" x 5½" piece. Cut out an octagon card on the fold. Cut yarn in 4" pieces. On the inside righthand page near the bottom of card, make dots to outline the word "DADDY." On the inside lefthand page, print "Thank You, God, for my Dad."

GO: Open card with fold at left. Glue eye in righthand page at top, with a heart seal under the eye. With a felt-tip pen trace the word "DADDY." Close the card and on the front glue 3 pieces of yarn and 3 balls of fringe to make balloons on strings.

NOTE: As children work on their Father's Day cards, allow them to talk about the things they do with their dads. You may want to ask the children what they like best about their dads. Then on the inside lefthand page under "Thank You, God, for my Dad" you can add what the child says. For instance, "Thank You, God, for my dad who plays ball with me."

TRACINGS

READY: Pictures of simple objects to make into patterns, pencils, sandpaper, typing paper, and crayons.

SET: Make patterns of simple objects by cutting them from sandpaper. On each piece of typing paper write, "God made the world and everything in it." Give each child a piece of typing paper, a pencil, and some crayons.

GO: Hold the pattern, sand side down, to the typing paper. Use a pencil to trace around it. This takes a little practice. Color your picture with crayons, trying to stay within the lines.

WITNESS MAGNET

READY: Bottle caps from vitamin bottles, 1½" tiles, scissors, small round magnets, rubber magnetic strips, glue, and religious seals.

SET: Trim seals to fit inside bottle caps or on tiles.

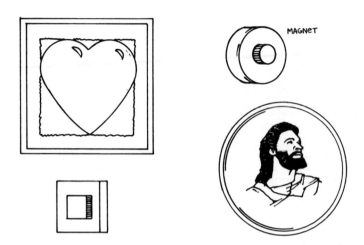

GO: Place some glue on top of bottle cap to glue a round magnet in place. Hold firm to dry. Cut a piece of magnetic strip and attach to back of tile. Inside bottle cap or on front of tile, glue and press seal. Use this as a gift for a very special person.

NOTE: Tiles are available from a tile store where they are sold by the sheet.

PATRIOTIC PENNANT

READY: Plastic straws, construction paper, glue, scissors, felt-tip pen, patriotic seals or pictures or both.

SET: Cut pennants from a 9" x 12" piece of construction paper. Each piece will yield three. (Each student will need two.) On one pennant print this Bible verse: "God is the King of all the earth" Psalm 47:7. Push one end of a straw into the end of another straw and secure with a little glue. This will make a pole 14½" long.

GO: Fold over 1" on the 4½" side of each pennant and glue on the edge, leaving a space in which you can insert the straw pole. Stick seals to the pennants or cut out patriotic pictures to fit pennants. Apply glue to the poles to keep them in place.

NOTE: For very small children, glue tabs made from paper to top and bottom on the 4½″ side and omit straw poles. There should be two pennants on the pole as shown.

SALAD FACES

READY: Oranges or canned pineapple, bananas, stuffed olives, lettuce, shoestring beets or red tomato, strawberries or raspberries, 6″ paper plates, knife, and forks for eating.

SET: Shred lettuce fine for hair (let children help). Peel and slice large oranges so each child has one large slice or use canned pineapple slices. Peel banana and cut thin slices, slice stuffed olives, strawberries or raspberries.

GO: Place an orange (or pineapple) slice in the center of paper plate for the face. Put lettuce around top for hair. Use a banana slice topped with a slice of stuffed olive for each eye. Place a strawberry or raspberry in position for the nose, and use a shoe-string beet or piece of tomato for the mouth. (You might want to take pictures of this craft, so the children can take it with them to create at home.) Pass out forks and napkins for eating. For a patriotic theme, add a small American flag.

NOTE: As the children eat their treat, talk about all of the wonderful foods God has given us to enjoy. Be sure to thank God for all of this good-tasting food.

CHINESE HAT

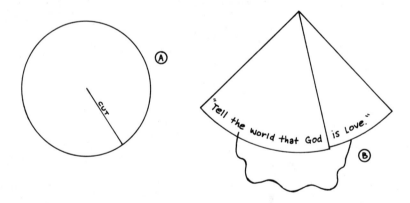

READY: 20″ circles of wallpaper (plastic-coated works best), scissors, crayons, and thin elastic.

SET: Cut into circle to center.

GO: Color hat with crayons, if desired. Along border write "Tell the world that God is love." Cross over cut lines to fit head. Staple or glue into place. Staple or tape on elastic chin band.

KEY SCRIPTURES

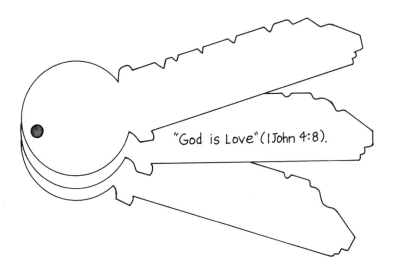

"God is Love" (I John 4:8).

READY: Construction paper, paper punch, paper fasteners, felt-tip pen or typewritten Scripture verses, glue, scissors, and crayons.

SET: As children learn their Scripture verses, they are given a key on which you have printed the verse, or a typewritten strip to glue to the key. Using a variety of colors, cut out enough keys for each child to have one key for each Bible verse to be learned.

GO: Color one side of the key with crayons. Your teacher will listen to you say your memory verse and then she will print it on the key, or she will give you a typewritten strip to glue to the key. When you have learned two verses, put your keys together with a paper fastener. See how many keys you can collect.

DIAMOND PENDANT

READY: Plastic-coated (no design) wallpaper, glue, scissors, yarn, and seals.

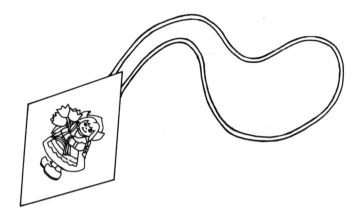

SET: Cut two diamonds 4″ x 2″ for each pendant. Cut a 30″ piece of yarn for each one. Make a variety of seals available.

GO: Glue the loose ends of the yarn between the 2 diamonds, placing the glue on the wrong sides of the wallpaper. Center your choice of seals on the diamond. (The seals may need extra glue.)

NOTE: To use as a name tag, print student's name and add "loves Jesus." If your class is large and you have new workers, keep name tags in the classroom for children to wear each week.

SHOE BOX CHURCH

READY: A small shoe box for each child, labels for windows and doors, a small box like an individual cereal box for the belfry, a toothpaste box for the steeple, toothpicks for the cross on the top, scissors, glue, and crayons or paint.

SET: Cut the self-stick labels for the door and arched side windows. If desired, spray paint the boxes (or let children color them).

GO: Color the box with crayons. Stick the door on one end of the shoe box. Stick 3 or 4 windows on each side of the box. Glue small box on top of shoe box near door end. On the top of the

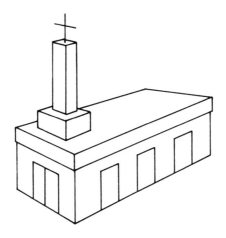

small box (belfry), glue the toothpaste box (steeple). Make a cross with two toothpicks and a little glue. Make a city of churches.

PIXIE HAT

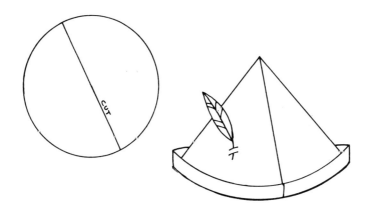

READY: Leftover wallpaper (plastic-coated is best), stapler, scissors, tape measure, and yarn, feathers, seals or ribbon.

SET: Mark a 18 to 20" circle on plastic-coated leftover wallpaper. Cut out and then cut in half.

GO: Overlap straight sides of half circle about 3". Staple together. Then turn up an inch on the edge and wear proudly. You may decorate the hat with yarn, feathers, seals, or ribbon.

DAYTIME SKY POSTER

God called the light "day," (Genesis 1:5).

READY: 9" x12" light blue construction paper, glue, seals for sun and aircrafts, cotton for clouds, kites cut from self-adhesive labels, scissors, string, and felt-tip pens.

SET: Collect materials and make available to students. Print on each sheet of construction paper, "God called the light 'day,'" Genesis 1:5.

GO: Glue on cotton for clouds. Stick on seals for sun and aircrafts. Cut kites from self-adhesive labels and stick on. Glue string to kite. With felt-tip pens make sun rays, raindrops, and anything you can see in the daytime sky.

NOTE: Decorate one wall or bulletin board inside your classroom with these posters.

RUBBINGS

READY: Onionskin paper, large crayons, coins, leaves, shapes cut from cardboard, typing paper, glue, and construction paper for frames.

SET: Cut from cardboard shapes such as butterflies, birds, flowers, trees, or other objects to illustrate a story and glue to the center of a piece of typing paper.

GO: Place coins, leaves, or shapes cut from cardboard on table. Place onionskin paper over these, and using side of a large crayon rub back and forth until design appears. To frame, glue to a larger sheet of construction paper.

NOTE: You may want to print on your students' finished product, "Work hard at whatever you do" taken from Ecclesiastes 9:10. Assure your students that God is pleased when they work as hard as they can to do the best job they can do.

APPLE PRAYER REMINDER

READY: 5½" x 5½" pieces of white construction paper, scissors, X-acto knife, crayons, green and brown construction paper, glue, felt-tip marker, paper punch, and yarn.

SET: Cut out apples from the 5½" x 5½" white construction paper. Cut heads and tails of worms from brown paper and mark features on them. Cut leaves from green paper. Cut slits in apple with X-acto knife for head and tail. Dot-to-dot selected message or Bible verse.

GO: Color the apple a light red. Glue head and tail of worm where shown. Print over teacher's message. Punch hole at top for hanging. Glue on a green leaf, if desired. Tie a yarn loop in the hole at top to hang.

NOTE: Instruct children to take home this prayer reminder and put it in a place they will see every day.

HELPING HANDS

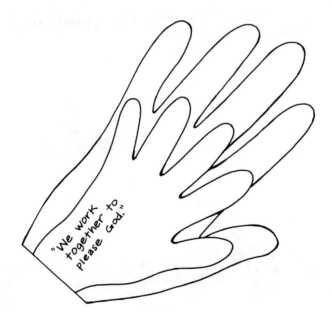

READY: Construction paper (2 colors), scissors, glue, and felt-tip pens.

SET: On dark construction paper draw around your hand with fingers spread. Cut one for each child. In class, help children draw around their hands on light-colored construction paper. After children have glued together the hands, print "We work together to please God" on the hands.

GO: Draw around your hand on a light-colored piece of construction paper. Your teacher will help you cut it out. Glue your hand to an adult's hand provided by your teacher.

NOAH'S ANIMALS

READY: 5½" x 8" meat trays, powdered sugar paste, cotton swabs, 3" x 5" cards, scissors, glue, stapler, light cardboard pieces 1" x 5", animal crackers, crayons, and yarn (optional).

SET: Cut the ark from the 3" x 5" card. Stand by to supervise further steps in making craft.

GO: Select 5 pairs of animals (nibble on the broken ones). Color the ark. Paste the animals in pairs around the outside of the meat tray using the powdered sugar paste and a cotton swab. With your teacher's help, make a spring from the 1" x 5" cardboard by folding it into fourths. Glue one end to the back of the ark and staple the other end to the meat tray. For a hanging plaque, punch hole in center top and add a loop of yarn.

FLOWER LEI

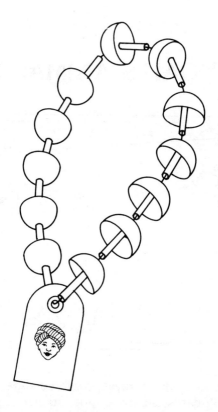

READY: 36" pieces of yarn, foam egg cups cut from egg cartons (12 for each lei), plastic straws, stringed tags, scissors, seals, and bobby pins for needles.

SET: Cut out and trim egg cups. With scissors point make a hole in the bottom center of each egg cup. Cut straws into 1⅞" pieces. Tie yarn to needle (bobby pin).

GO: String cups and straws alternately on yarn. Tie tag to center of lei and tie ends of yarn together. Use "share" seals on one side of tag and "children of the world" seals on the other side. You may adapt to other themes by changing the seals.

PRAISE THE LORD HARP

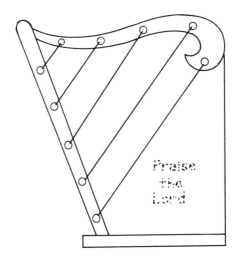

READY: 8½" x 10" construction paper, 40" of colored yarn, scissors, bobby pins for needles, paper punch, felt-tip pens, and crayons.

SET: Cut out harps as shown. Punch five holes on top and left side of harp. Write "Praise the Lord" in broken lines for children to trace.

GO: Color harp, trying to stay within the lines. Thread the yarn into the bobby pin and tie to hold. Sew so the yarn makes the strings of the harp. Trace the letters.

SCARECROW PUPPET

READY: Brown paper lunch bags, newspaper, construction paper, material scraps, 6″ paper plate, 5 ounce paper cup, scissors, glue, and rubber bands.

SET: Cut eyes, noses, and mouths from construction paper. Cut small material patches.

GO: Glue on the eyes, nose, and mouth. Glue on some patches of material. Fill sack with one double sheet of newspaper crumpled into a loose ball. Secure neck with a rubber band to make a handle. Glue a paper cup upside down on the back of a small paper plate. Glue on top of head for hat. Let the puppets talk to each other.

A GREAT FISH

READY: 4½″ x 8″ foam meat trays, scissors, crayons, curly ribbon, and paper punch.

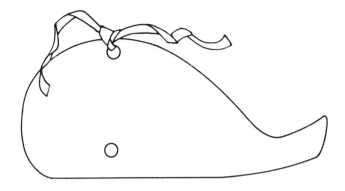

SET: Cut fish (whale) shape from tray.

GO: Color fish with crayons. Punch hole for eye and spout. Tie a piece of curly ribbon in spout and curl it. Hold by ribbon that you have tied in the spout hole. In a breeze, it will look like the fish is swimming.

NOTE: Using their fish, let students retell the story of Jonah.

SEA POSTER

READY: 9" x 12" light green construction paper, crayons, felt-tip pens, and seals of ships or boats, fish and frogs.

SET: Draw a horizon line across middle of paper that looks like waves.

GO: Remembering that ships and boats go above the waves and the creatures of the sea go below the waves, stick the seals where they belong. You may wish to draw some fish or boats to add to your sea poster.

DECORATING CHAINS

READY: Colored construction paper, string, stapler or glue.

SET: Give each child 2 pieces of construction paper 1" wide and 13" long and 2 pieces 1" wide and 9" long. Use colors that fit in with your decoration color scheme.

GO: Glue or staple the ends of the long strip together. Also glue or staple it in the center. Then slip the small strip into the bottom of the figure eight and out the center of the top. Repeat the process with the other strips of paper. Attach them together with a stapler. Add a piece of string for hanging.

SMILING FACE HAND PUPPET

READY: 6" paper plates, stapler, yarn, crayons or construction paper, facial features, and glue.

SET: Each face will require 1½ paper plates. Cut yarn into 1" pieces for hair. Make construction paper facial features, if desired.

GO: Staple 1/2 plate to full plate with insides together. On outside of full plate place eyes, nose, and mouth either by drawing and coloring them or glueing ones made from construction paper. Place glue around the top of the plates for hair. Add yarn hair to glue. To work the hand puppet slip your hand in the pocket made when you stapled the plates together.

TEPEE

READY: Plastic straws, lightweight cardboard 6" x 12", glue, stapler, and scissors.

SET: Cut on solid lines and fold on dotted lines as shown.

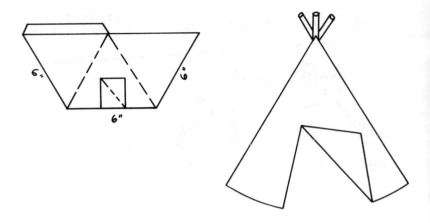

GO: Color one side of tepee with crayons or decorate with seals. Glue straws on fold lines on inside, allowing straws to extend at top. Let dry. Lap so tab is on inside, glue and let dry. Open flap and staple or glue back to make entrance.

NOTE: For a mission display make an Indian village.

"EYES" BOOK

Thank You, God, for

to see.

"EYES" BOOK

READY: Construction paper, large movable eyes, pen, glue, pictures, scissors, and yarn.

SET: For each book cut a large piece of construction paper in half. Fold into fourths, accordion style. On front make broken lines to spell out "THANK YOU, GOD, FOR O-O's TO SEE". Cut yarn into 18" lengths. Cut pictures of things children like from magazines. Cut several for each child to glue into his book.

GO: Fill in dotted lines and glue on movable eyes. Attach an 18" piece of yarn to hold book closed. On the inside paste pictures from magazines of things you like.

THANKSGIVING TURKEY COOKIES

READY: Sugar cookies (3" or 4" in size), a can of chocolate frosting, candy corn, small size peanut butter cups, chocolate chips, red licorice rope, and cotton swabs for dabbing frosting.

SET: Spread newspaper on the table and give each child a cookie, a peanut butter cup, a chocolate chip, 6 pieces of candy corn and 1″ piece of red licorice rope.

GO: Put a small dab of chocolate frosting on the flat side of each piece of corn. Press them on the cookie around the top to make tail. In the center of the cookie place another dab of frosting and press the peanut butter cup upside down. Place a dab of frosting on top of peanut butter cup and add a chocolate chip and the red licorice rope. Transport in a small plastic bag.

SPACE POSTER

READY: 9″ x 12″ black construction paper, seals such as stars, circles for sun and moon, other seals for spacecrafts and planets, one large, bright star for the first Christmas, and felt-tip pens.

SET: Collect all materials and have available for students.

GO: Place seals on black paper in any order. Some might like to draw space-things on another piece of paper, cut it out and glue it in place.

NOTE: Space is a very interesting part of God's creation. Allow children to ask questions about it as they work. Then thank God for giving us space to enjoy.

CHRISTMAS WREATH NAME PLATE

READY: 6″ paper plates, stiff paste made with powdered sugar and a little water, cotton swabs, spearmint candy leaves, red gumdrops, nativity seals or small Christmas card pictures of the nativity, glue, and felt-tip marker.

SET: Prepare paste using one cup of powdered sugar and enough water to make a stiff paste. Dot-to-dot with felt-tip marker child's name on a paper plate as shown.

GO: Paste eight spearmint leaves on the paper plate to form a wreath. Paste two red gumdrops at the top. In the center place a seal and using a felt-tip marker, trace your name. (If seals are unavailable, glue a small picture from a Christmas card.) Let dry.

NOTE: Use this edible craft as a place card at a Christmas party or dinner.

STORY SCROLL

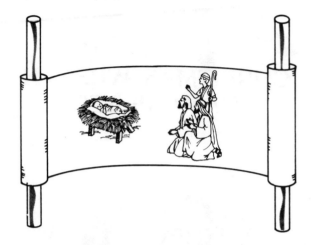

READY: Plastic straws, adding machine tape, glue, scissors, rubber band, and seals or felt-tip pens.

SET: Cut the plastic straws into 2 pieces and the adding machine tape into 18″ lengths.

GO: Glue a piece of the plastic straw to each end of the 18″ strip of tape. Stick on the seals in sequence from left to right. (If seals are unavailable, have students draw their own pictures.) Roll up from each end. Secure with a rubber band.

NOTE: Use Christmas seals for the Christmas story and use animal seals to tell the story of Noah's ark.

CHRISTMAS CARD PUPPETS

READY: Old Christmas cards with large pictures of people from the first Christmas, craft sticks, glue, scissors, and envelopes.

SET: Cut out characters, making one set for each child. A set should include angels, baby Jesus, Mary and Joseph, shepherds, and Wise-men.

GO: Glue sticks to bottom back of people.

NOTE: As the teacher tells the story of Jesus' birth, the children hold up the proper character. Each child can take them home in an envelope to share Jesus' birth with those at home.

NEW HELP FOR PRESCHOOL TEACHERS

Classroom Story and Activity Books

Parables Jesus Told, *2444*
Bible Animals, *2445*
Bible Babies, *2446*
Bible Children, *2447*
Favorite Bible Stories, *2448*
Jesus Is Born, *2449*

Each book contains six lessons with activity sheets for eight students to use as a unit or to supplement other materials. Available now at your local Christian bookstore or Standard Publishing.